COPYRIGHT © 2023 JCPUBLISHING

ADULT COLORING DRAGONS VOLUME 2

ENJOY COLORING 25 SPECTACULAR, FANTASTICAL IMAGES OF DRAGONS,

COLLECTED IN THIS SET IN VOLUME 2

ISBN: 9798372092730

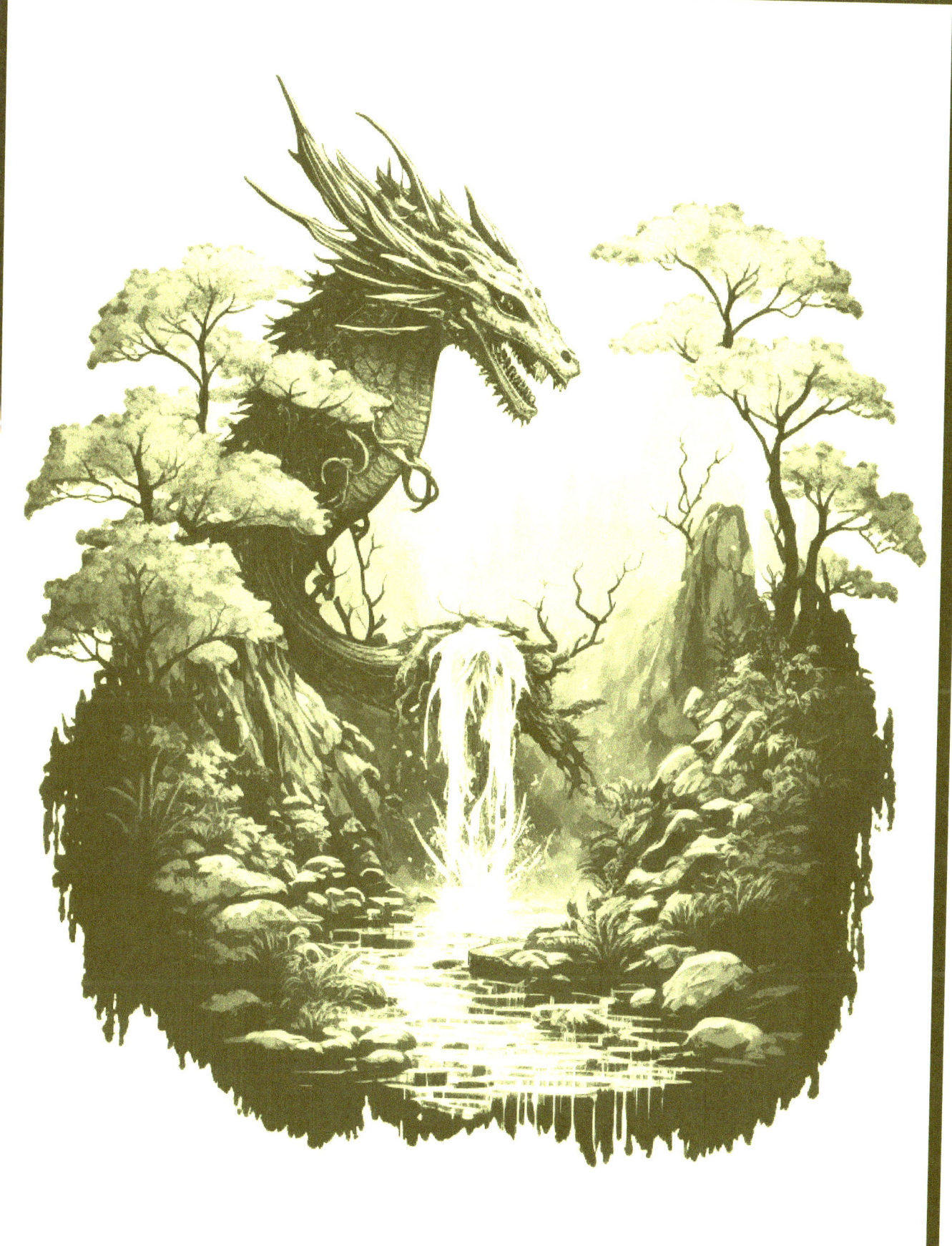

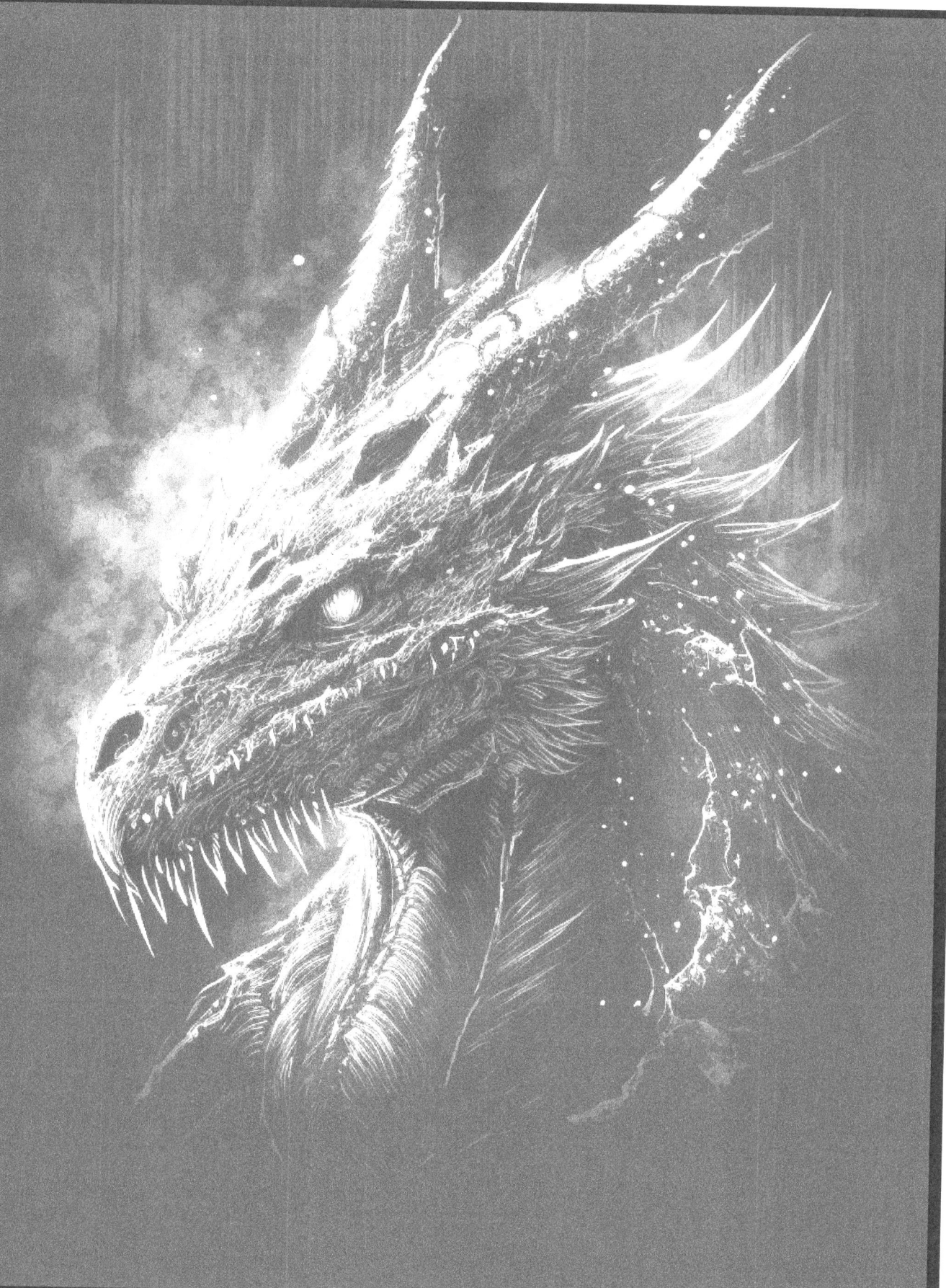

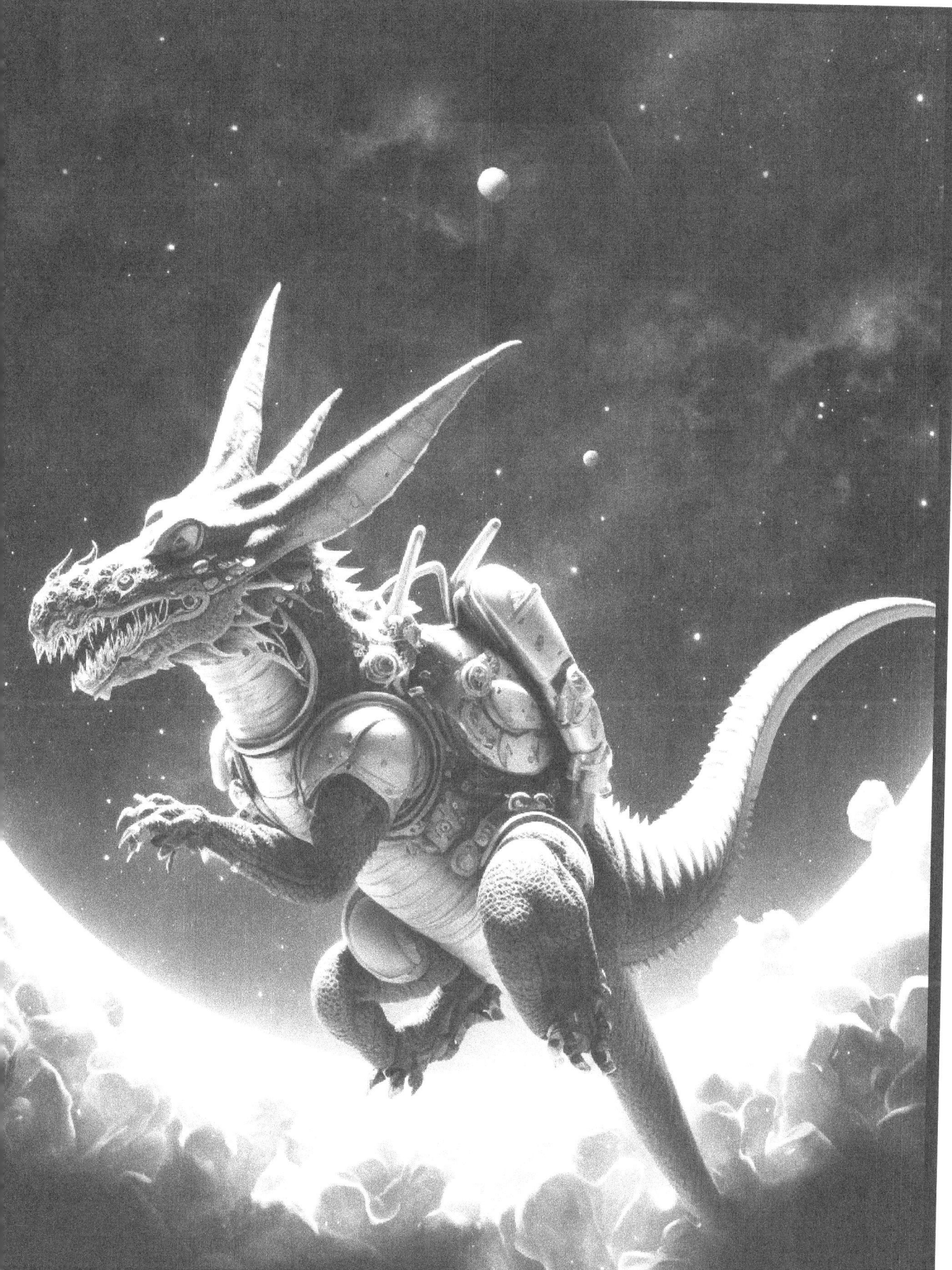

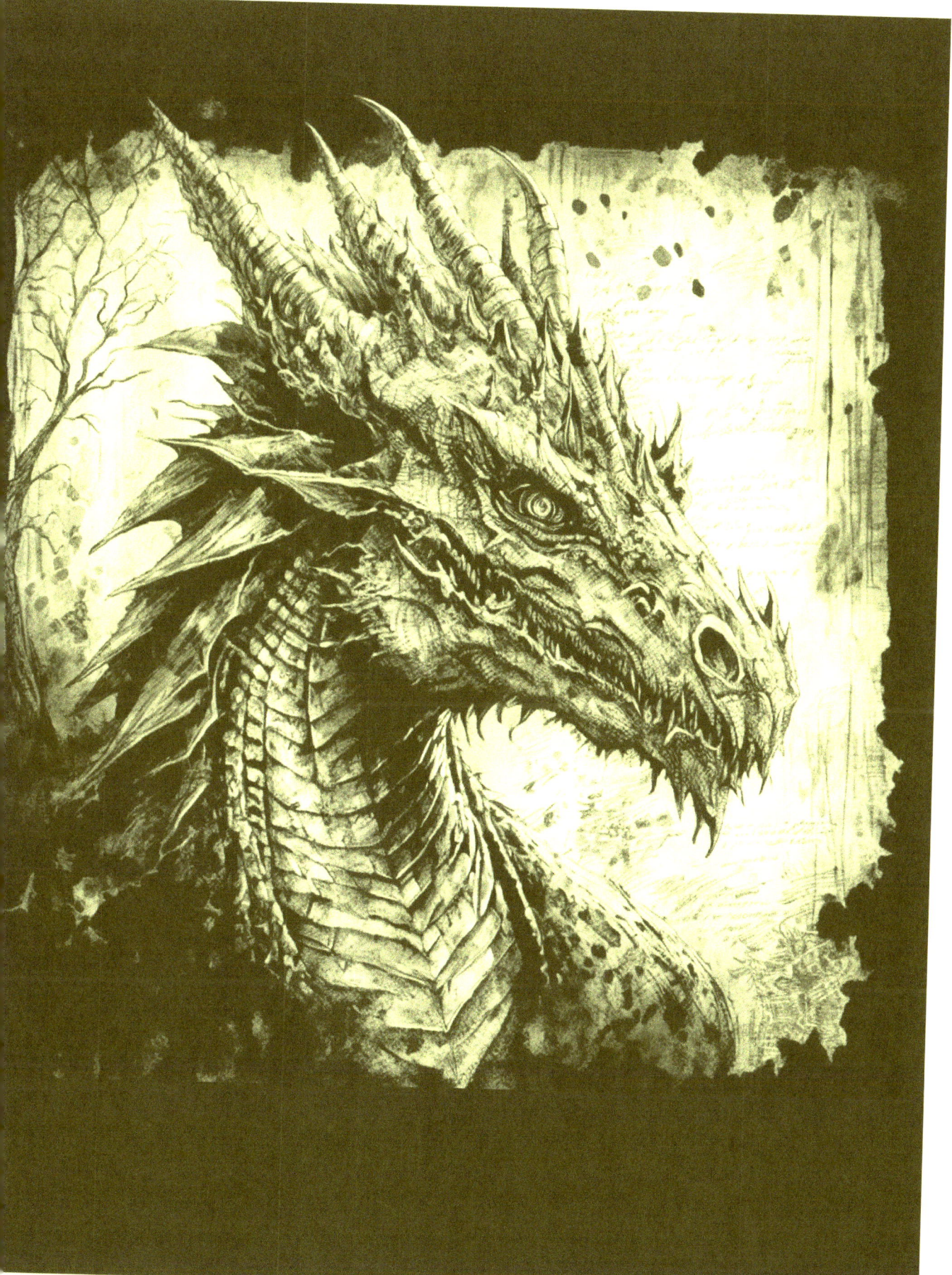

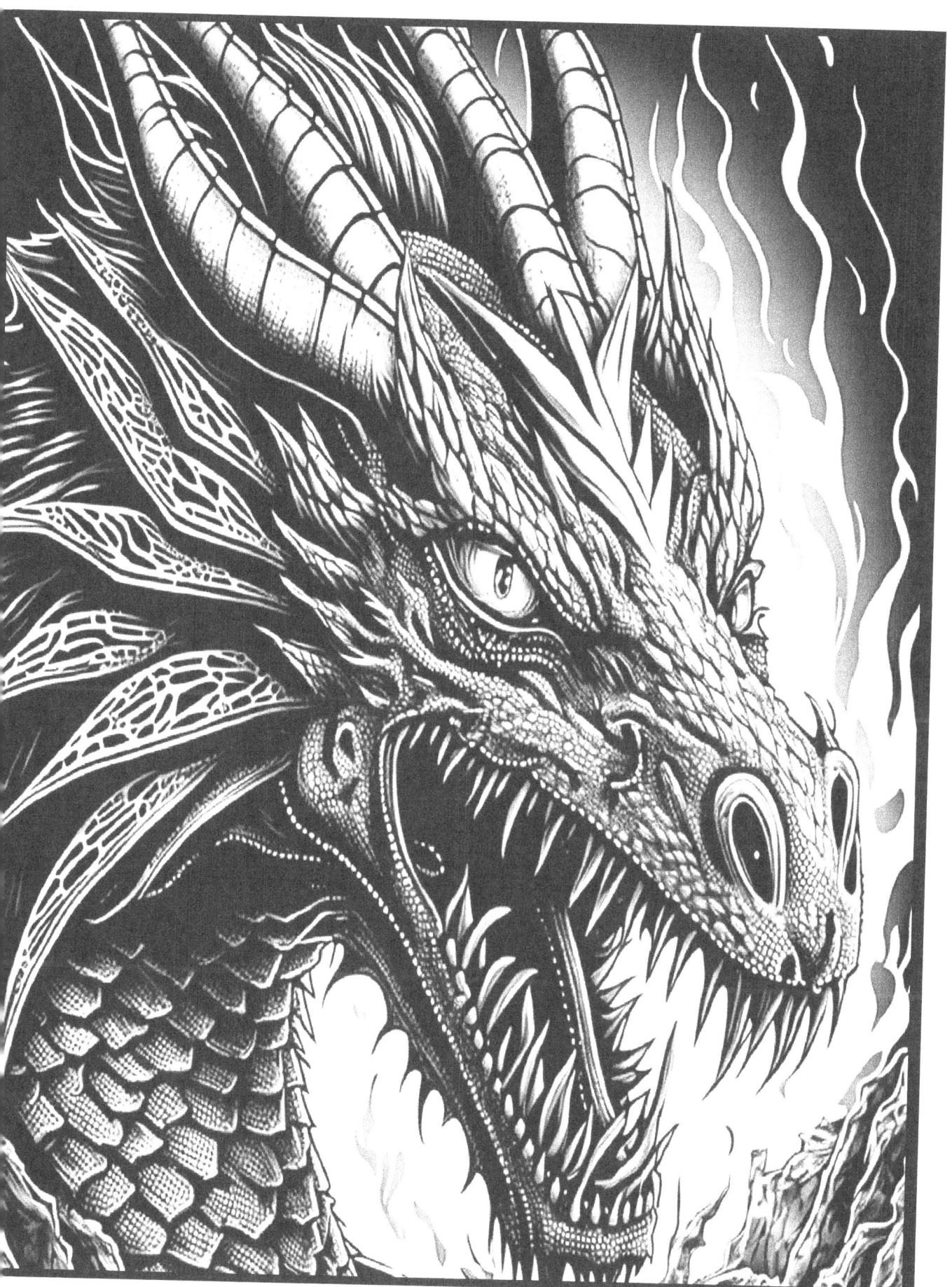

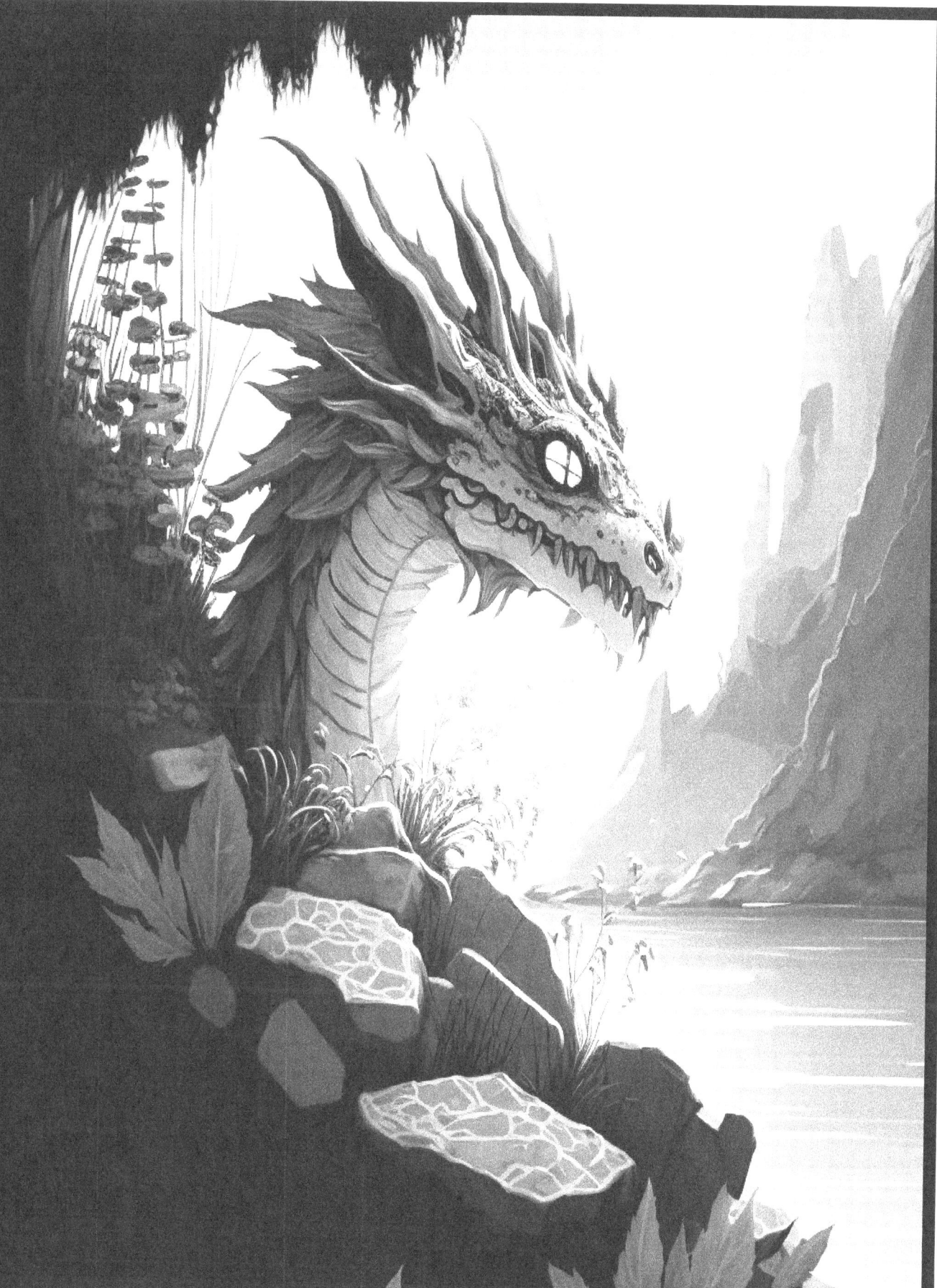

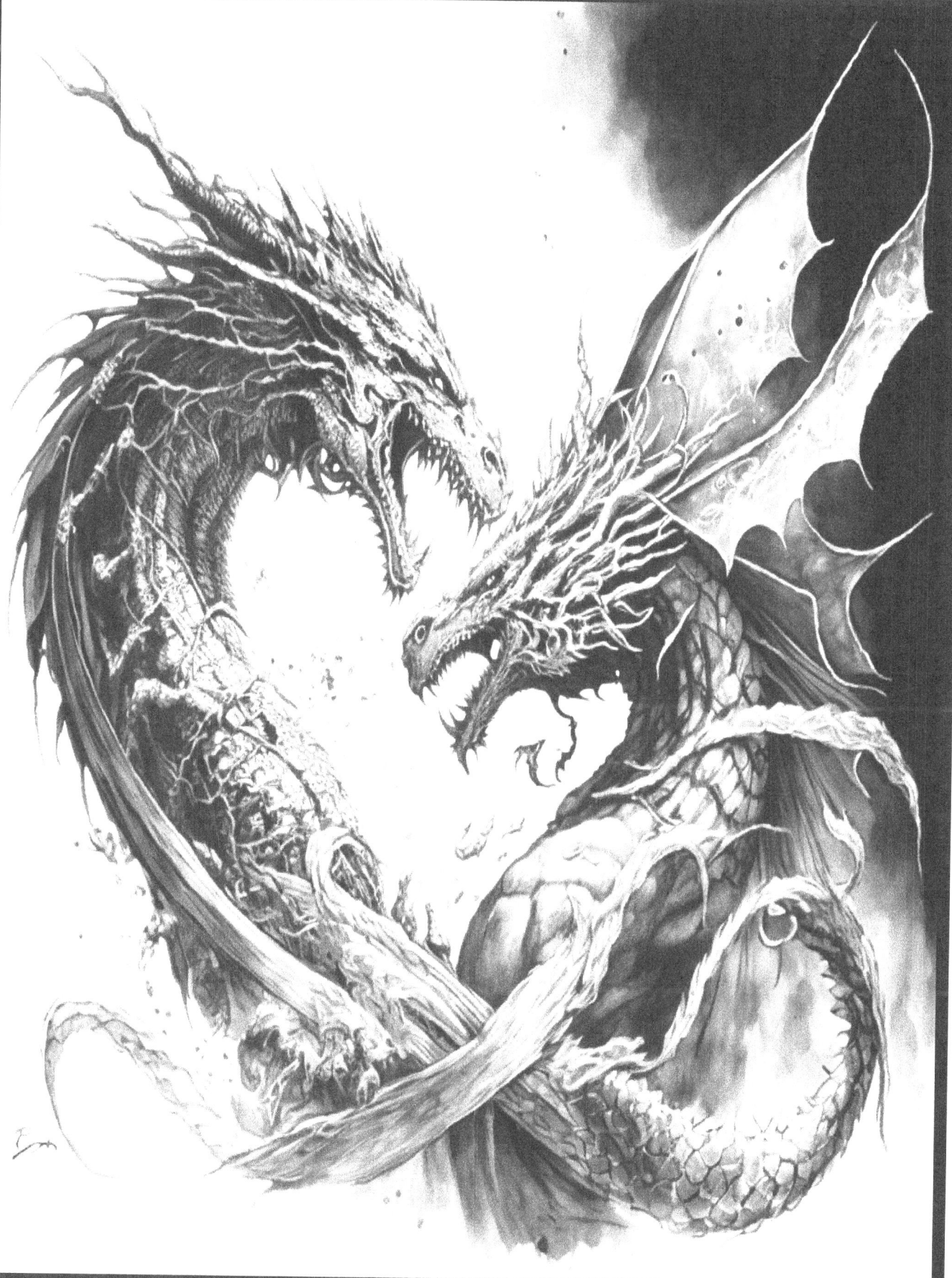

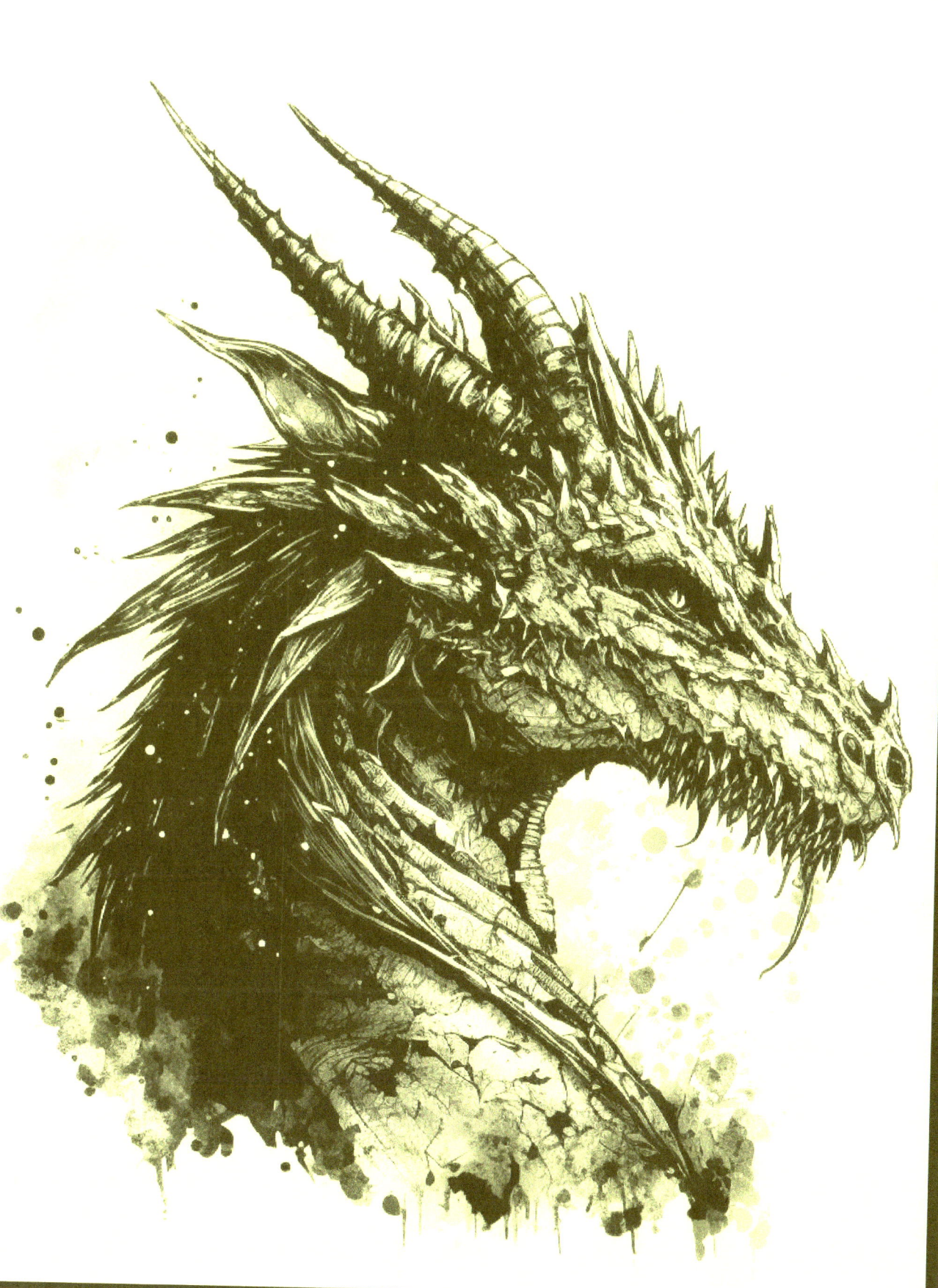

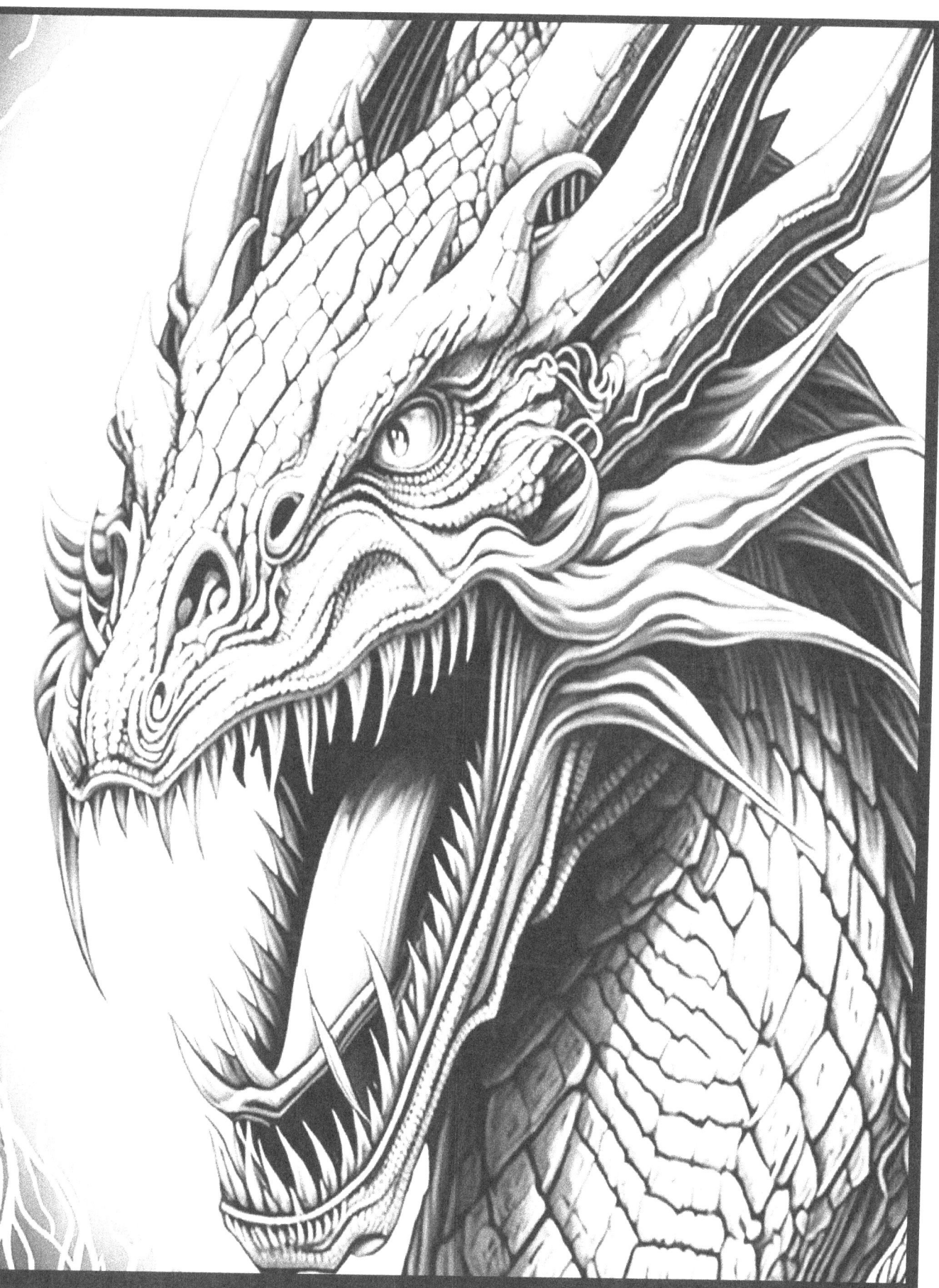

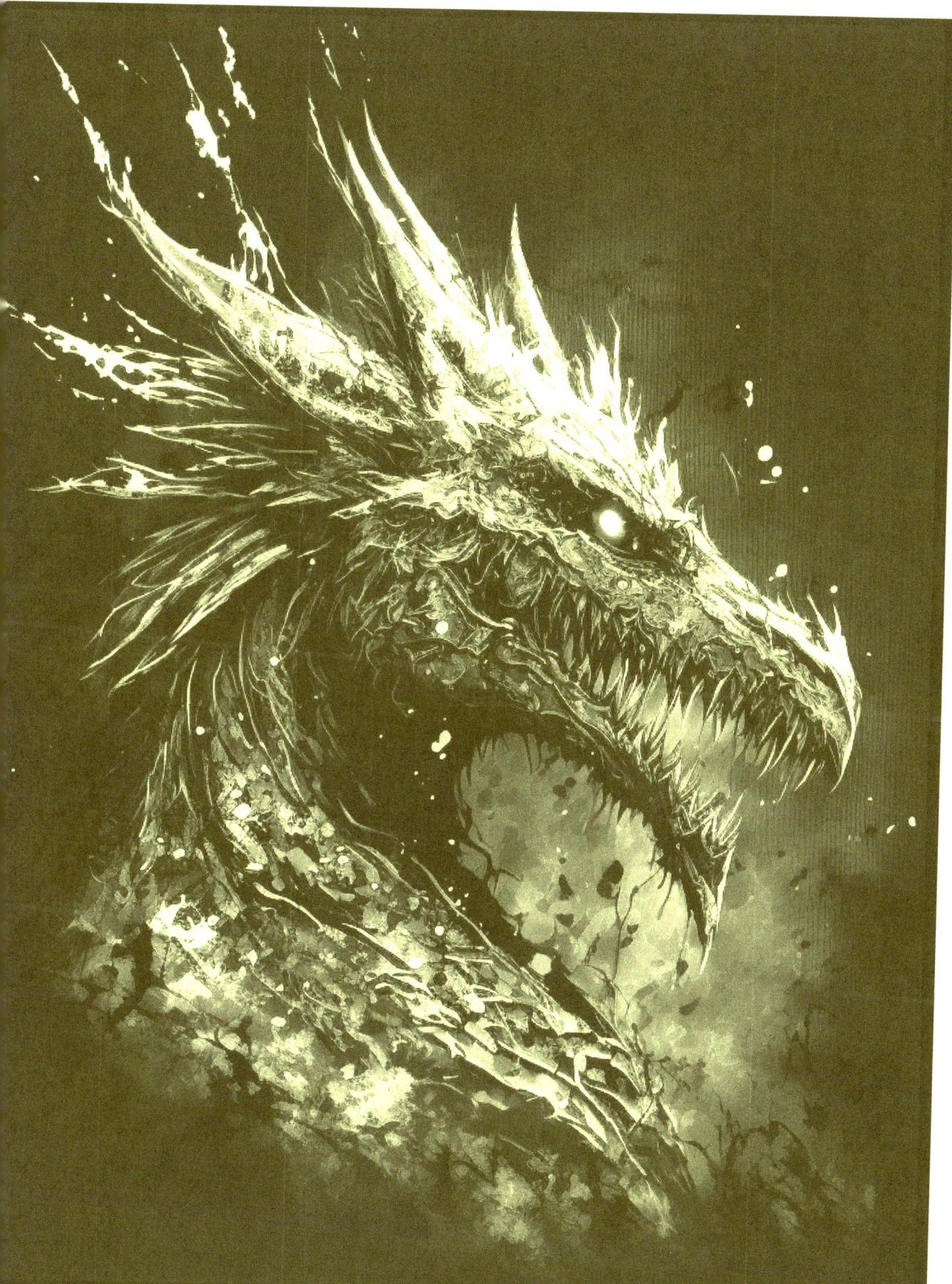

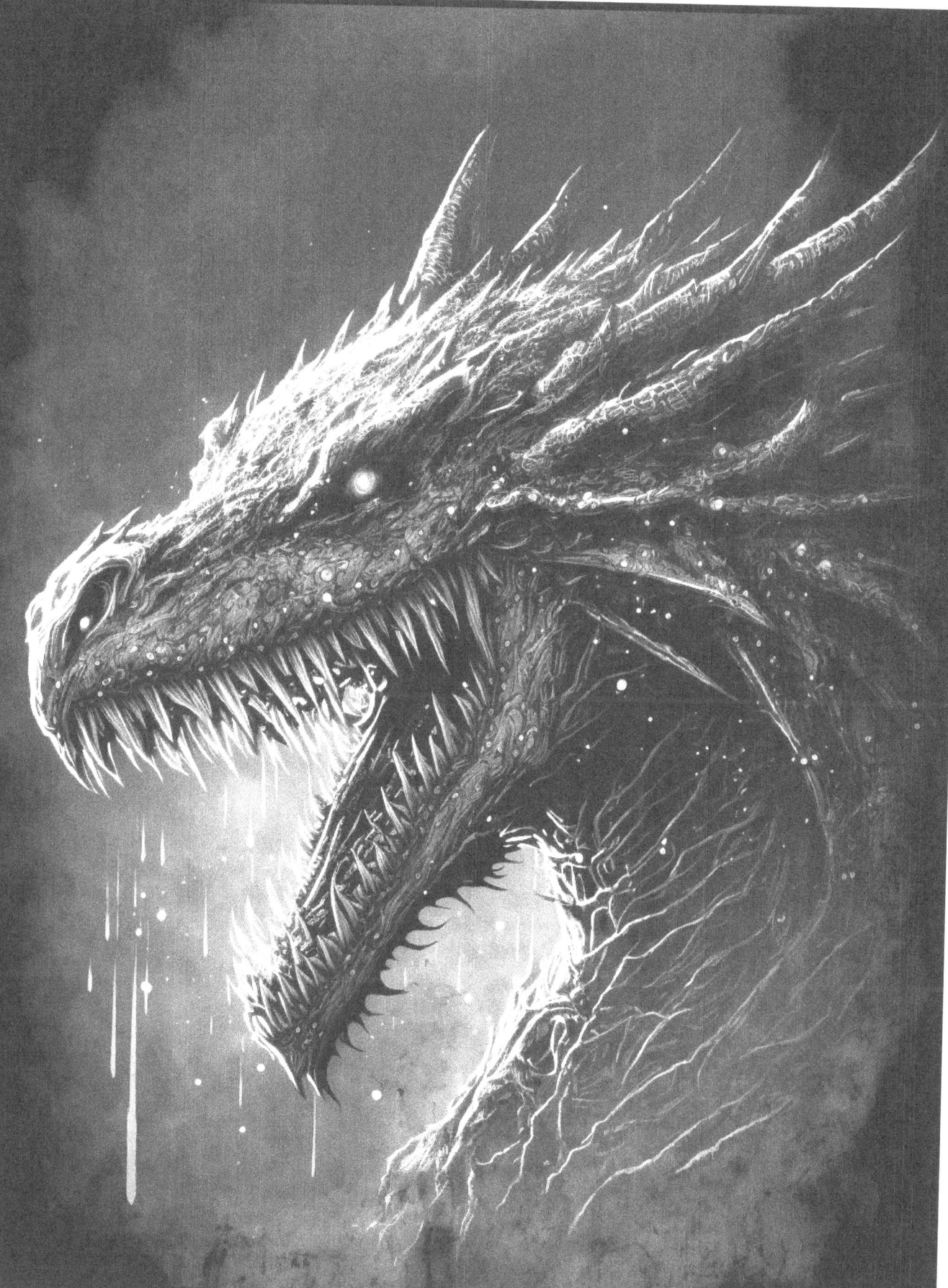

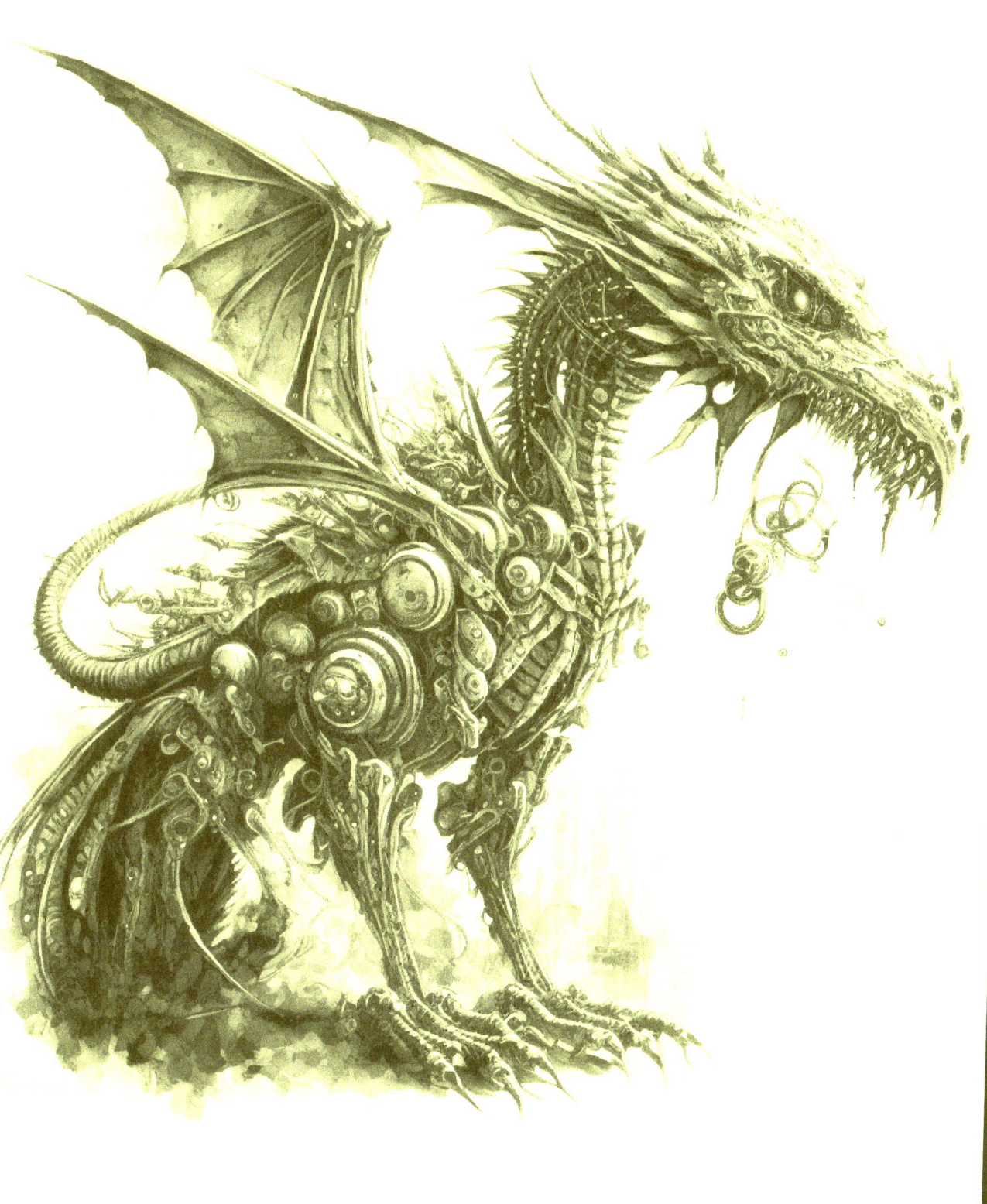

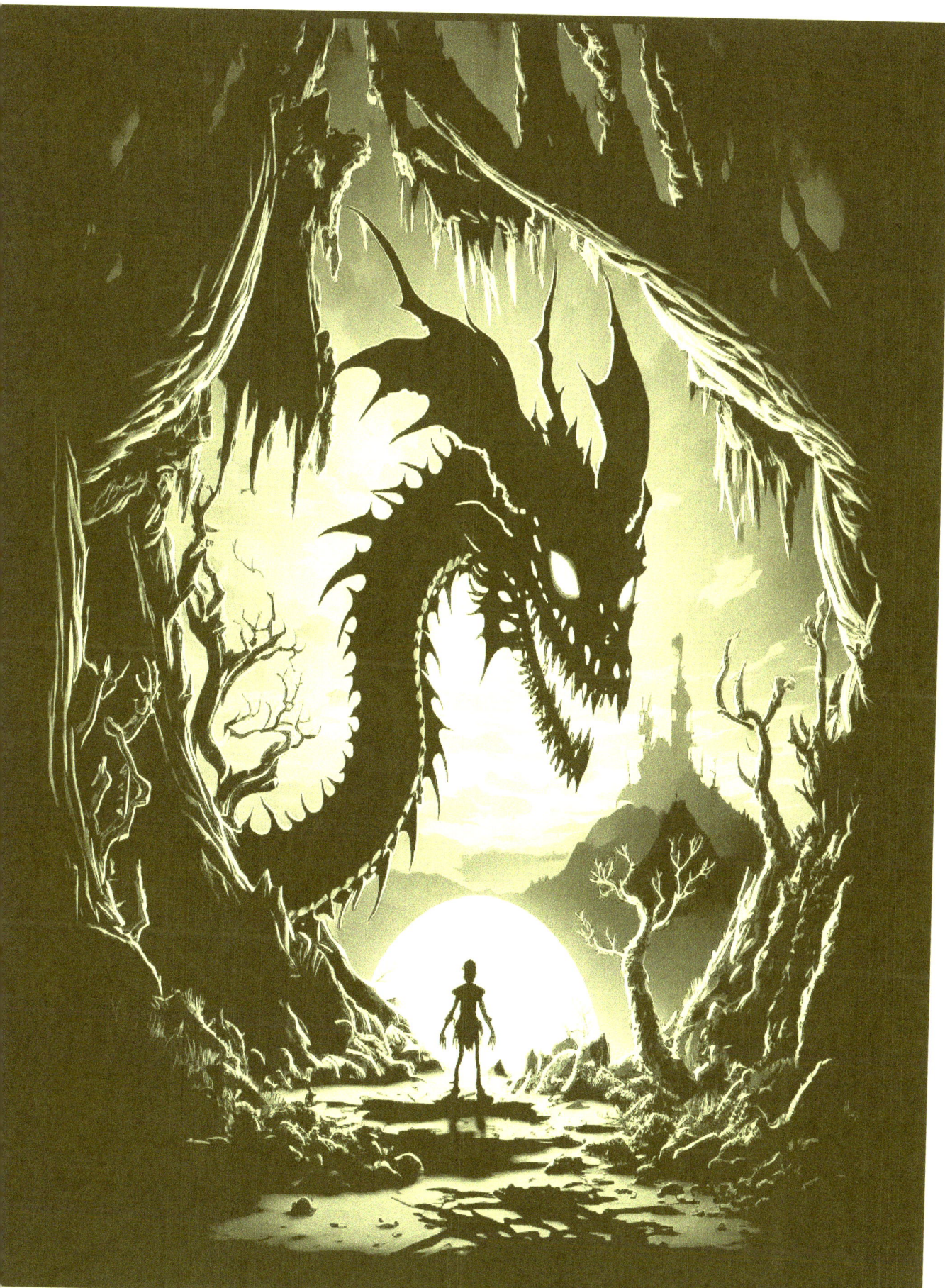

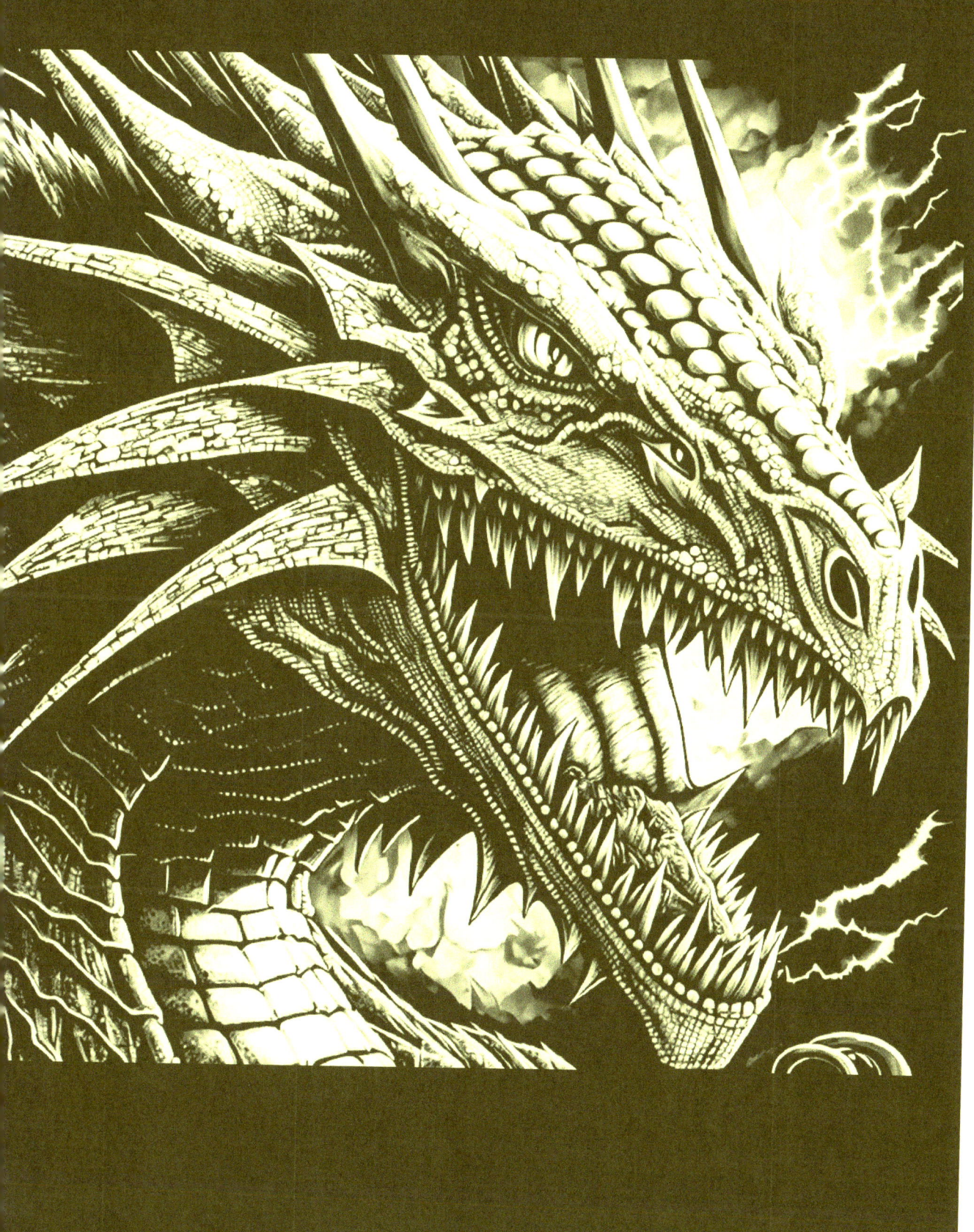

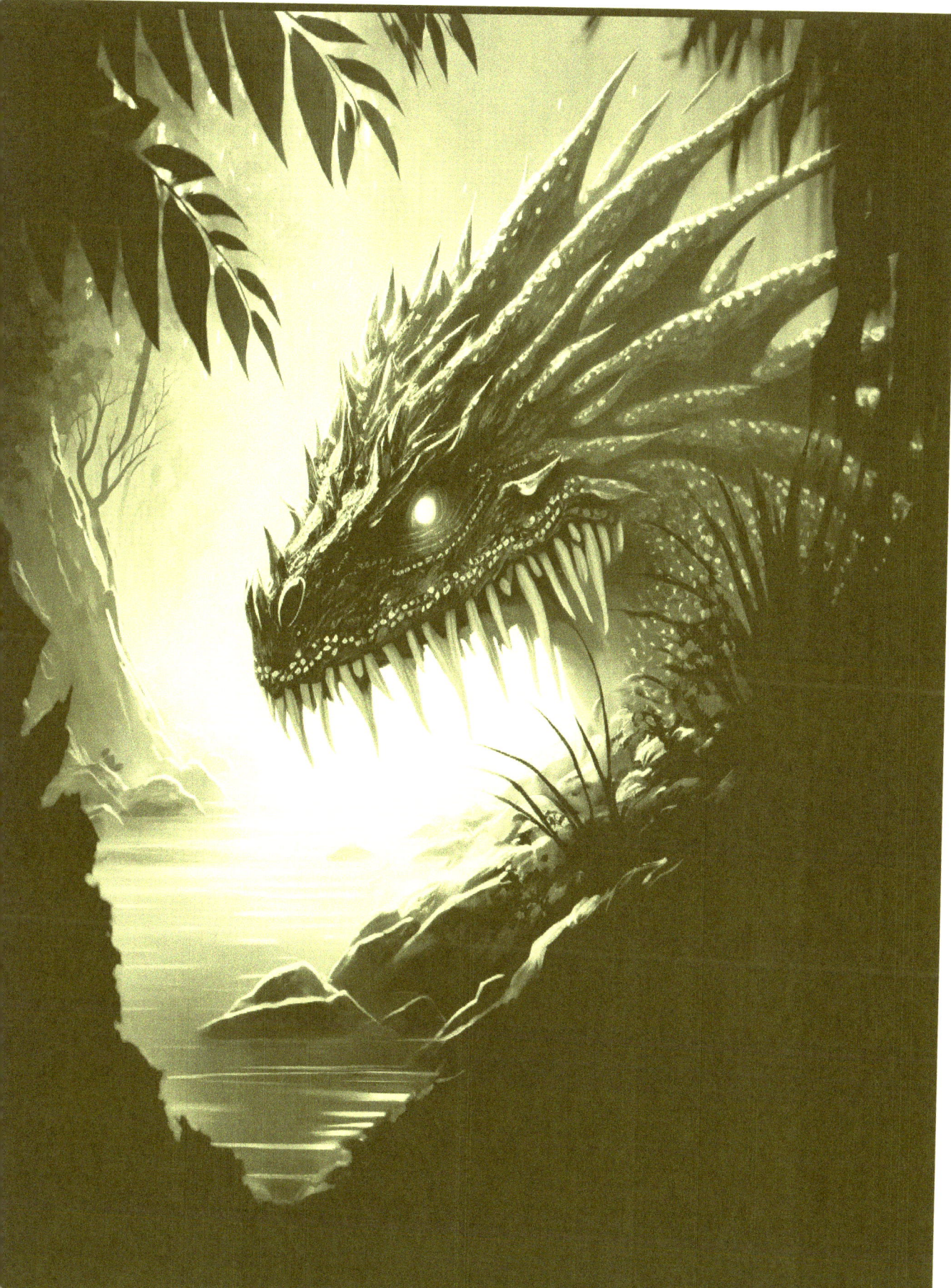

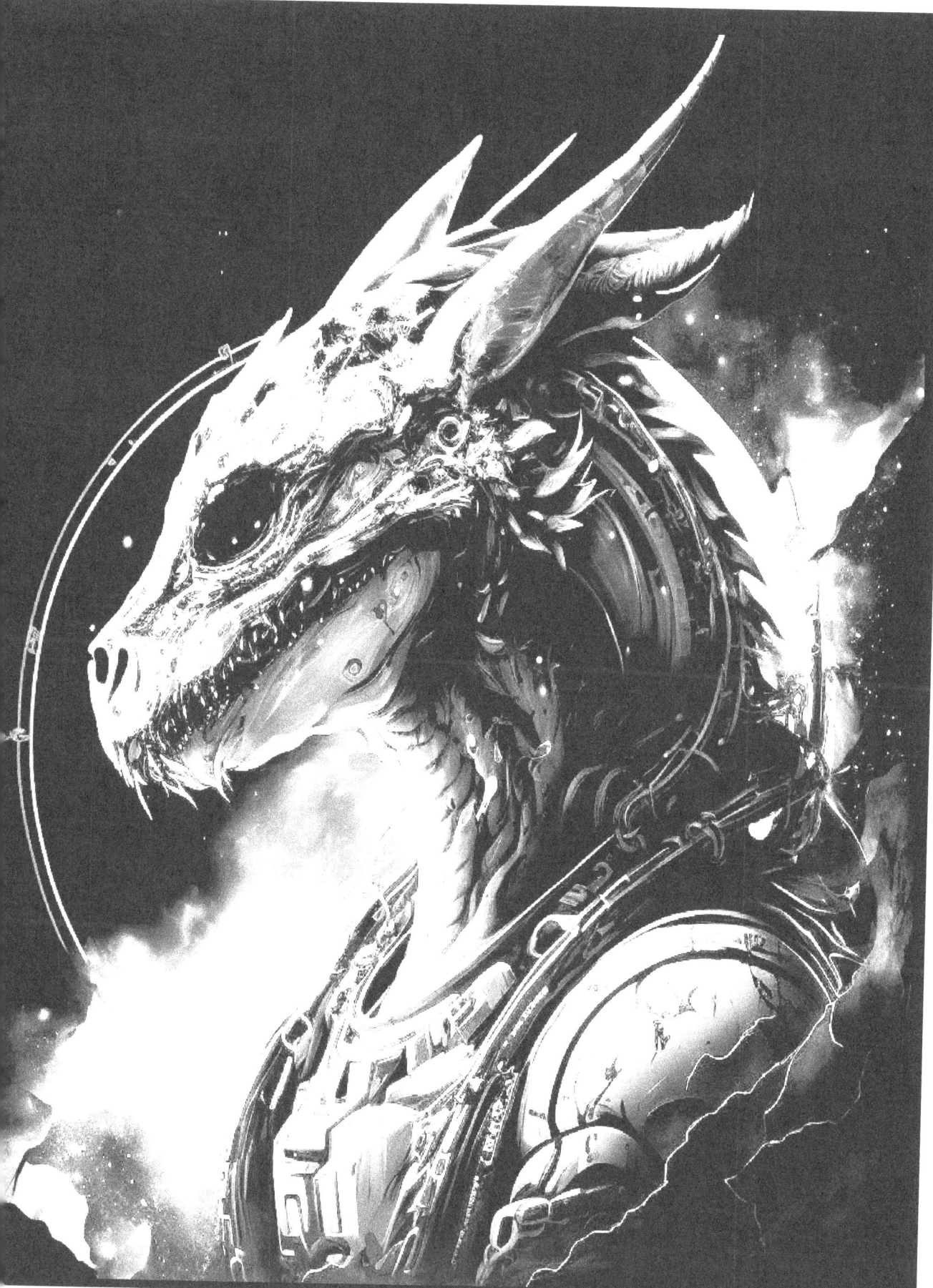

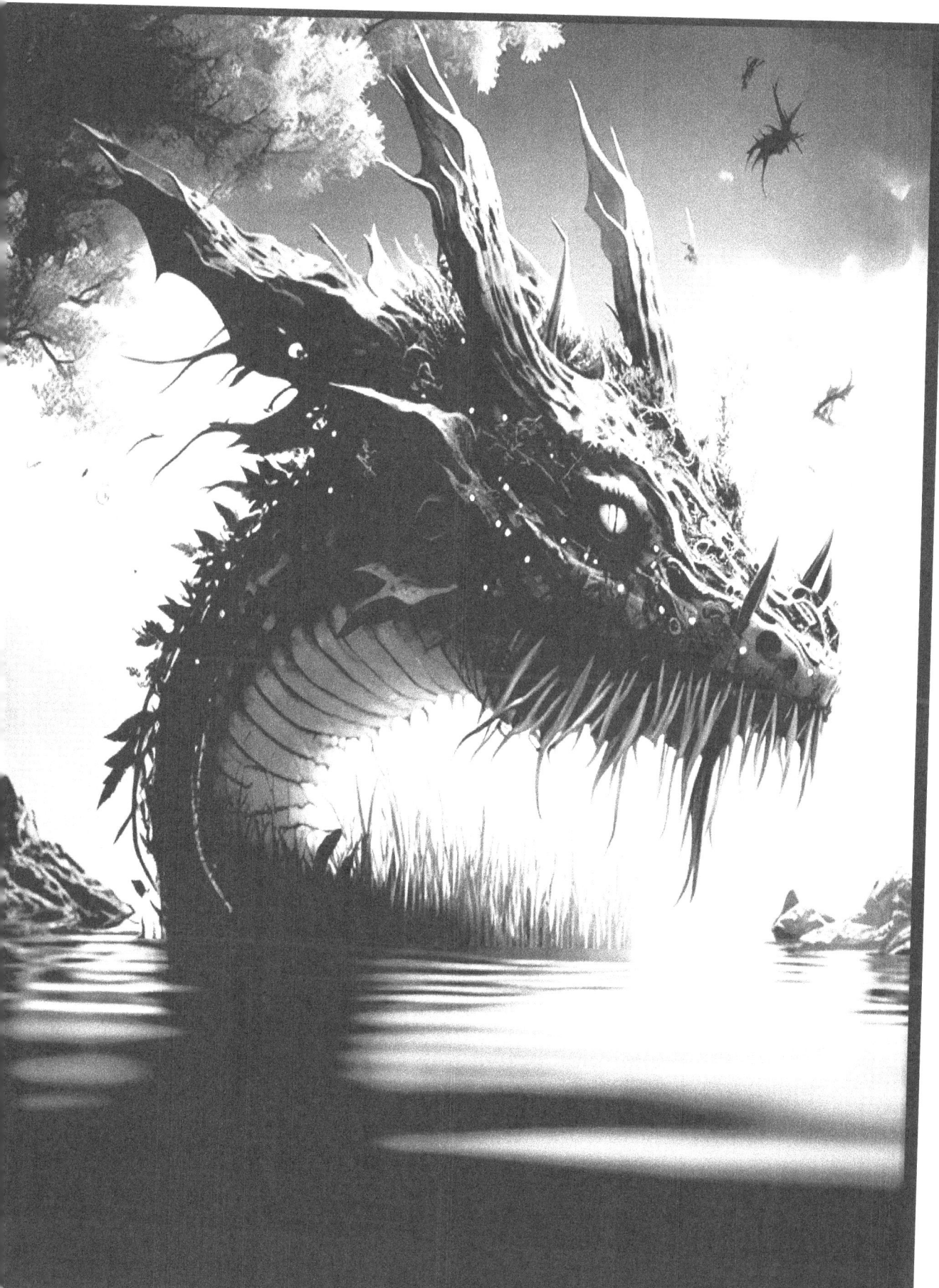

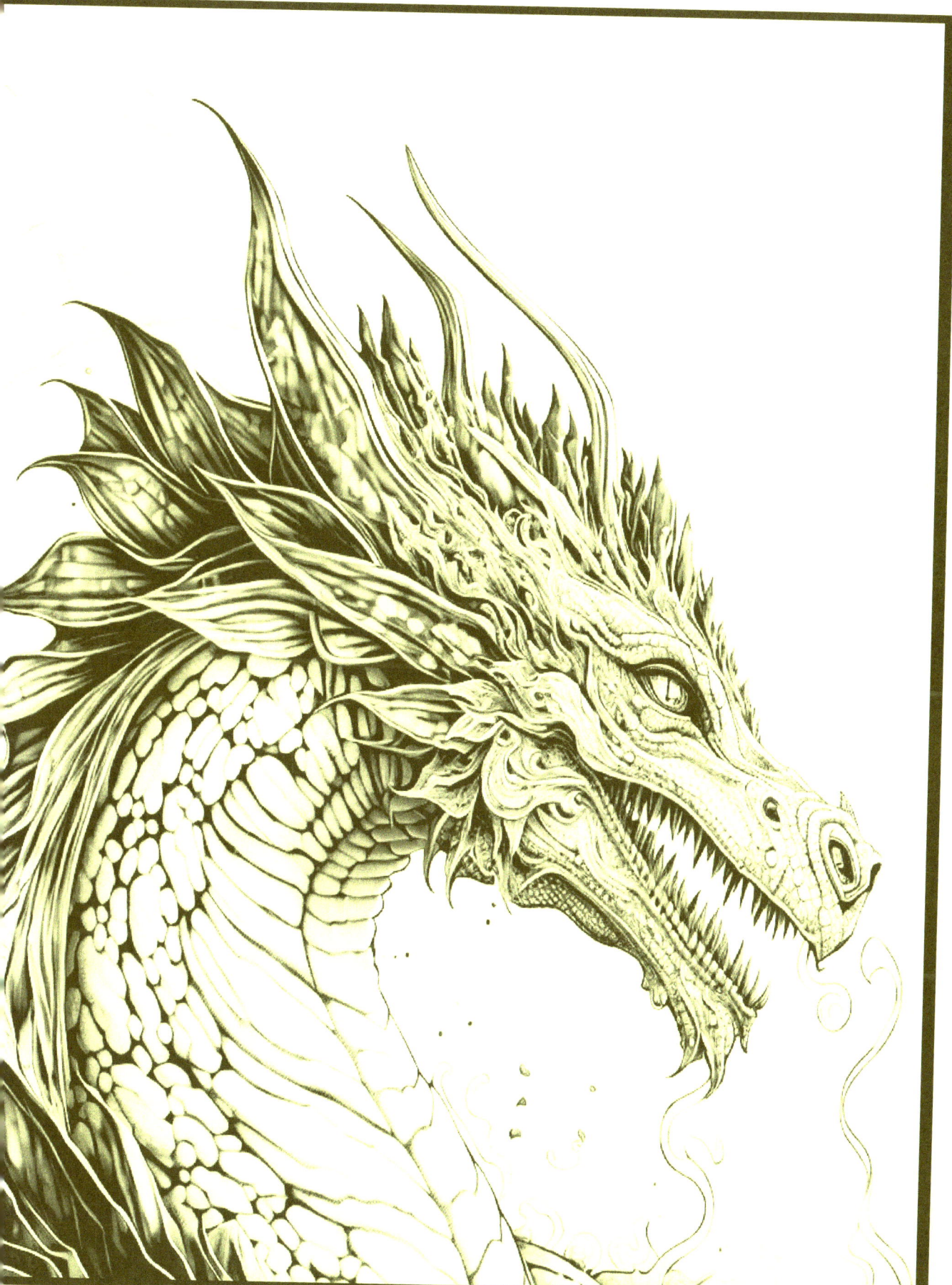

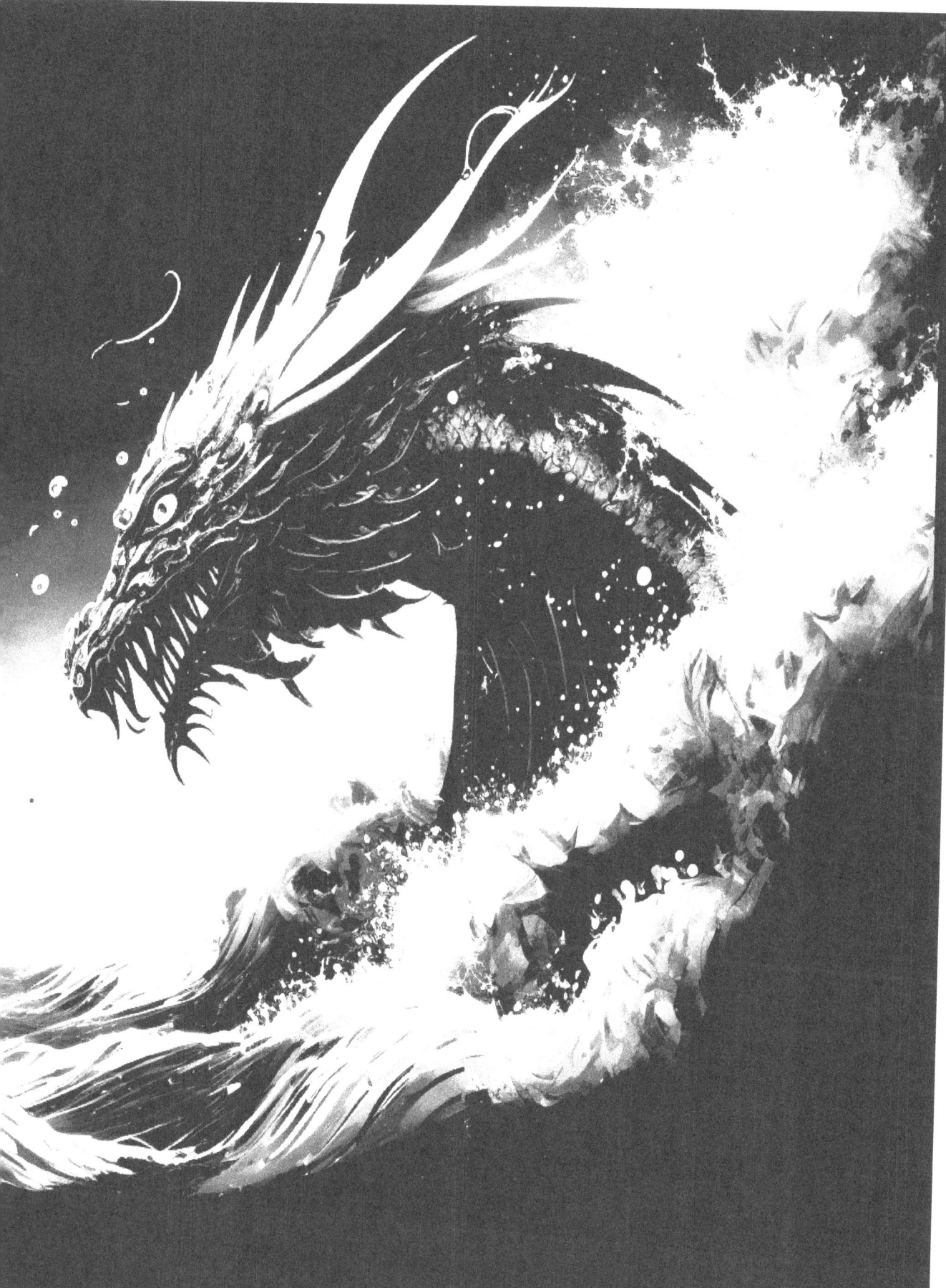

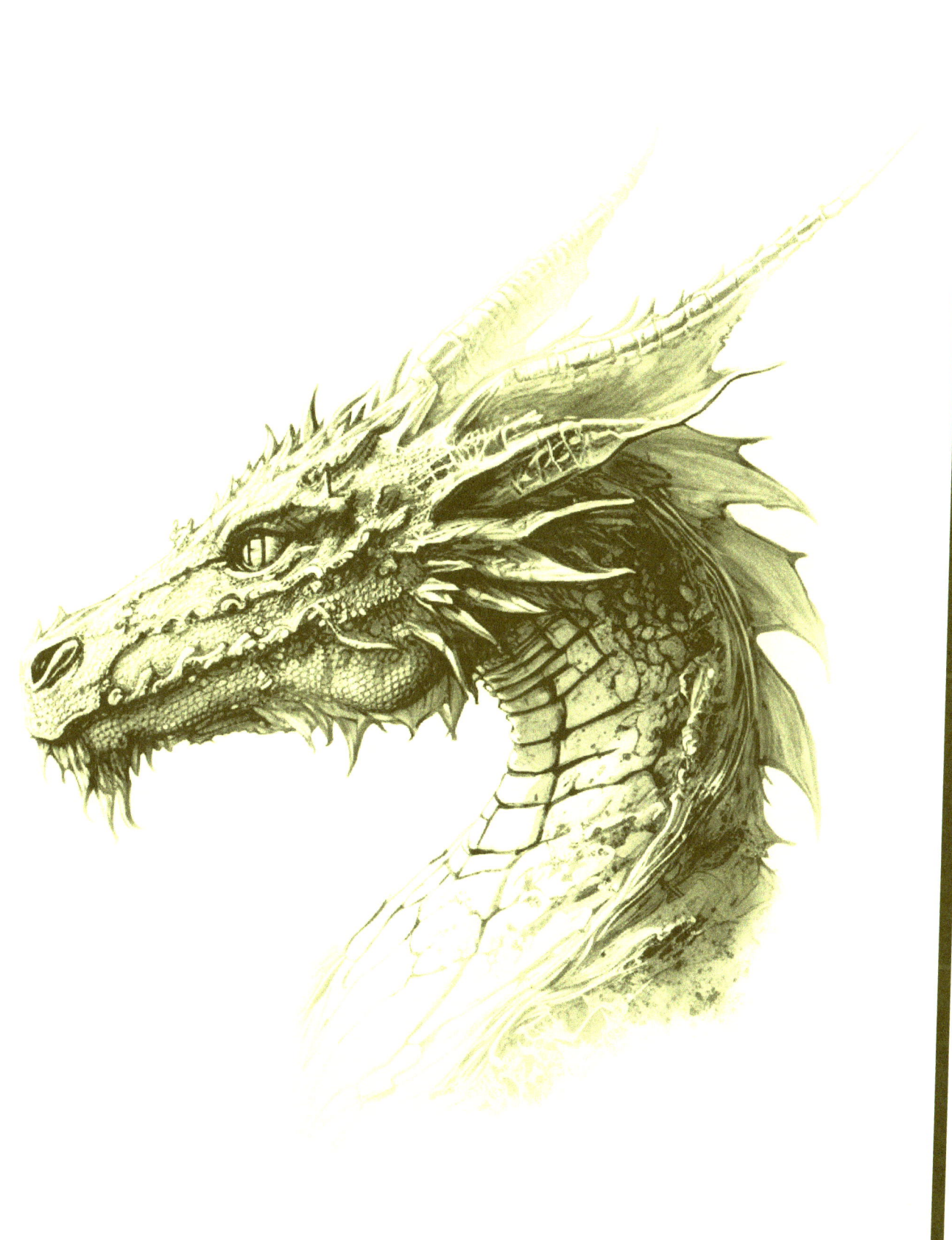

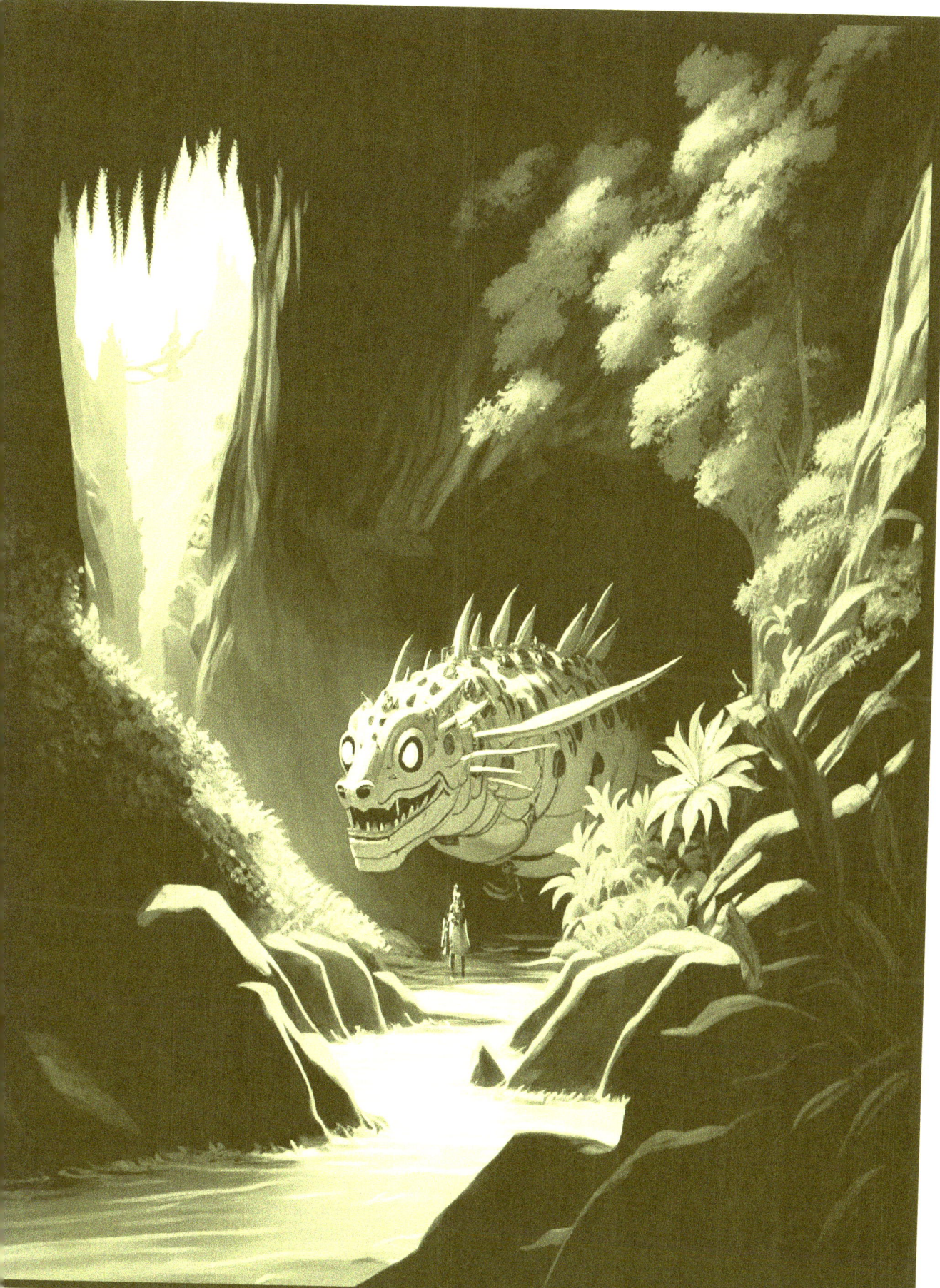

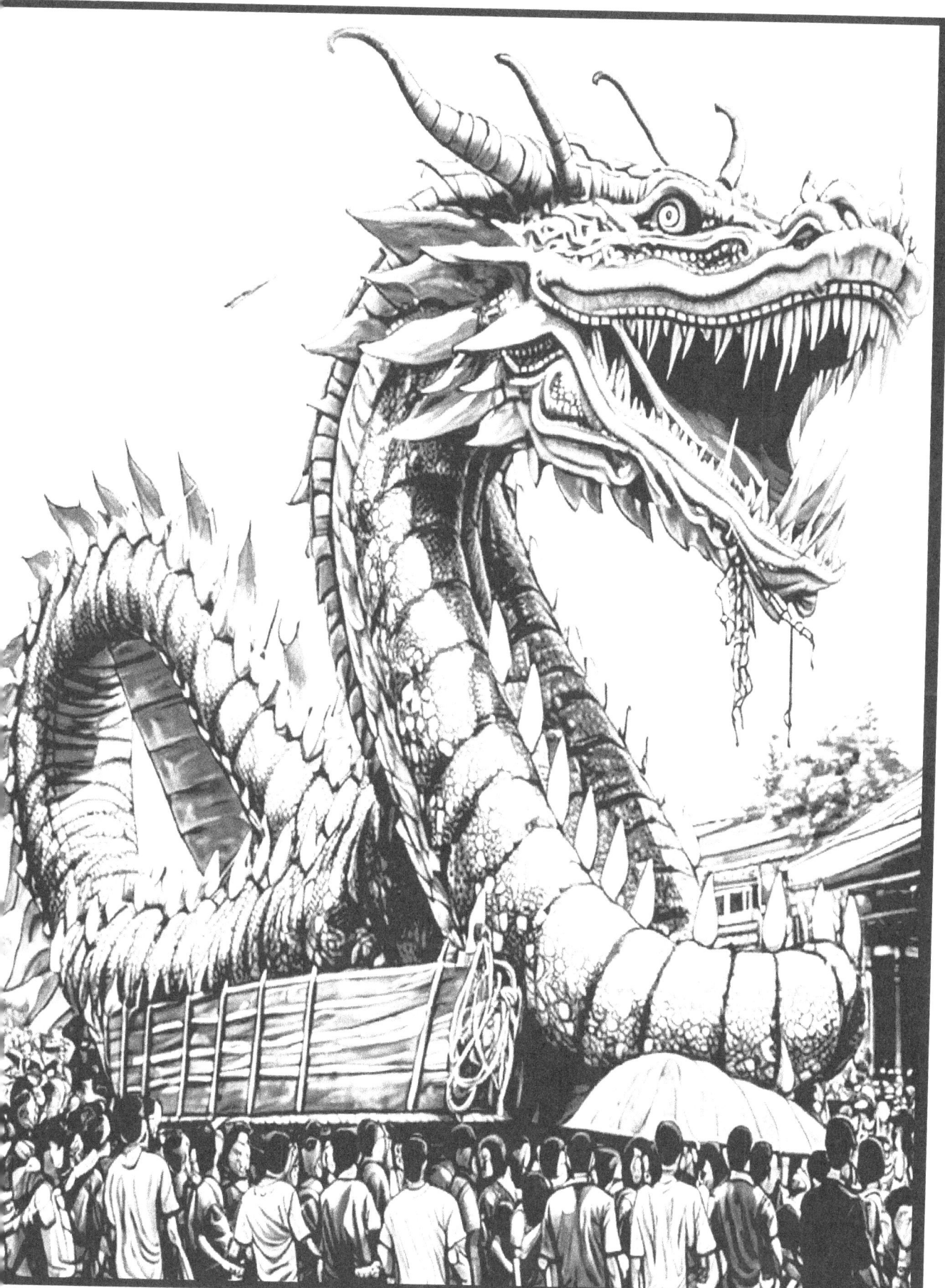

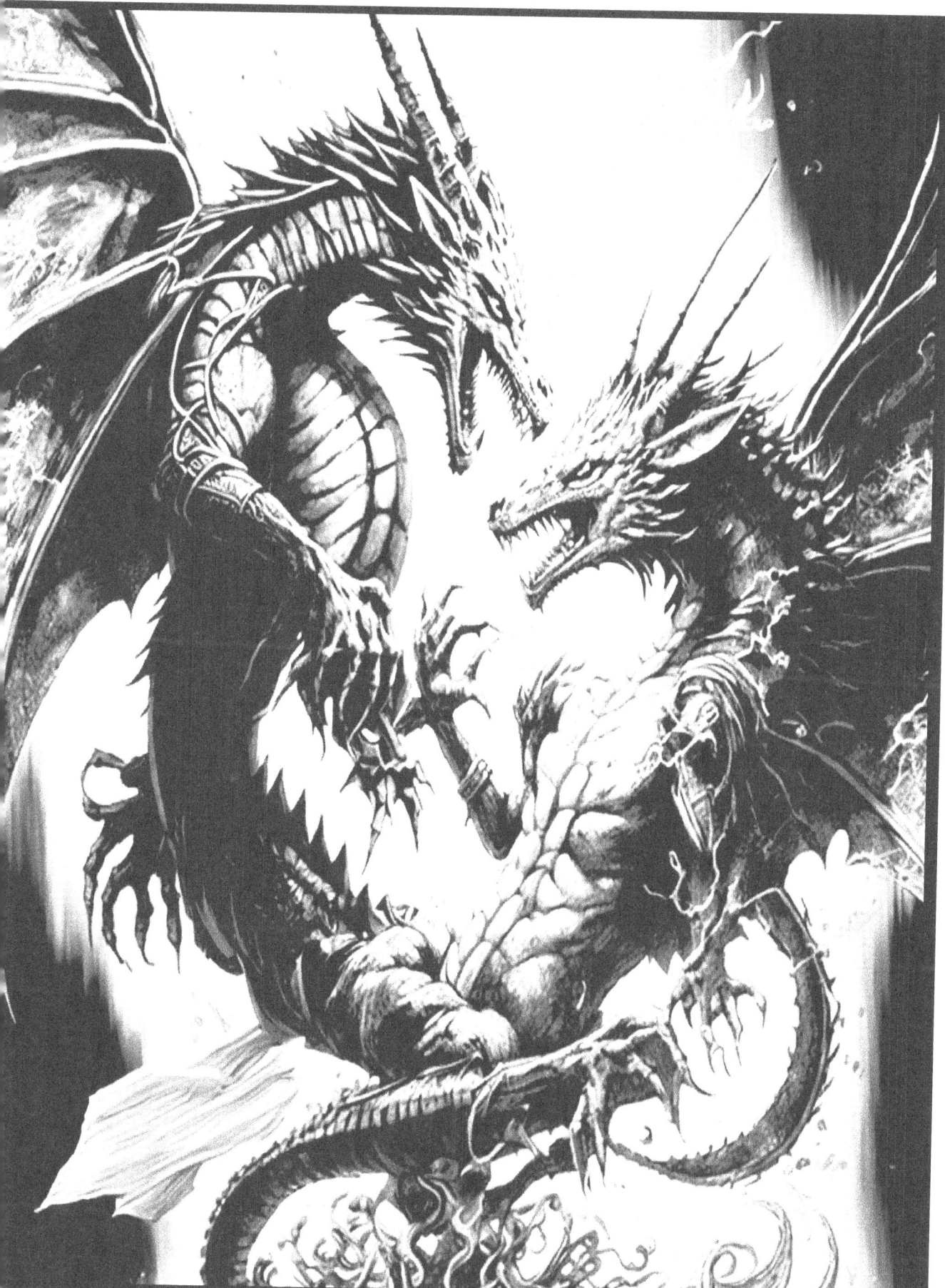

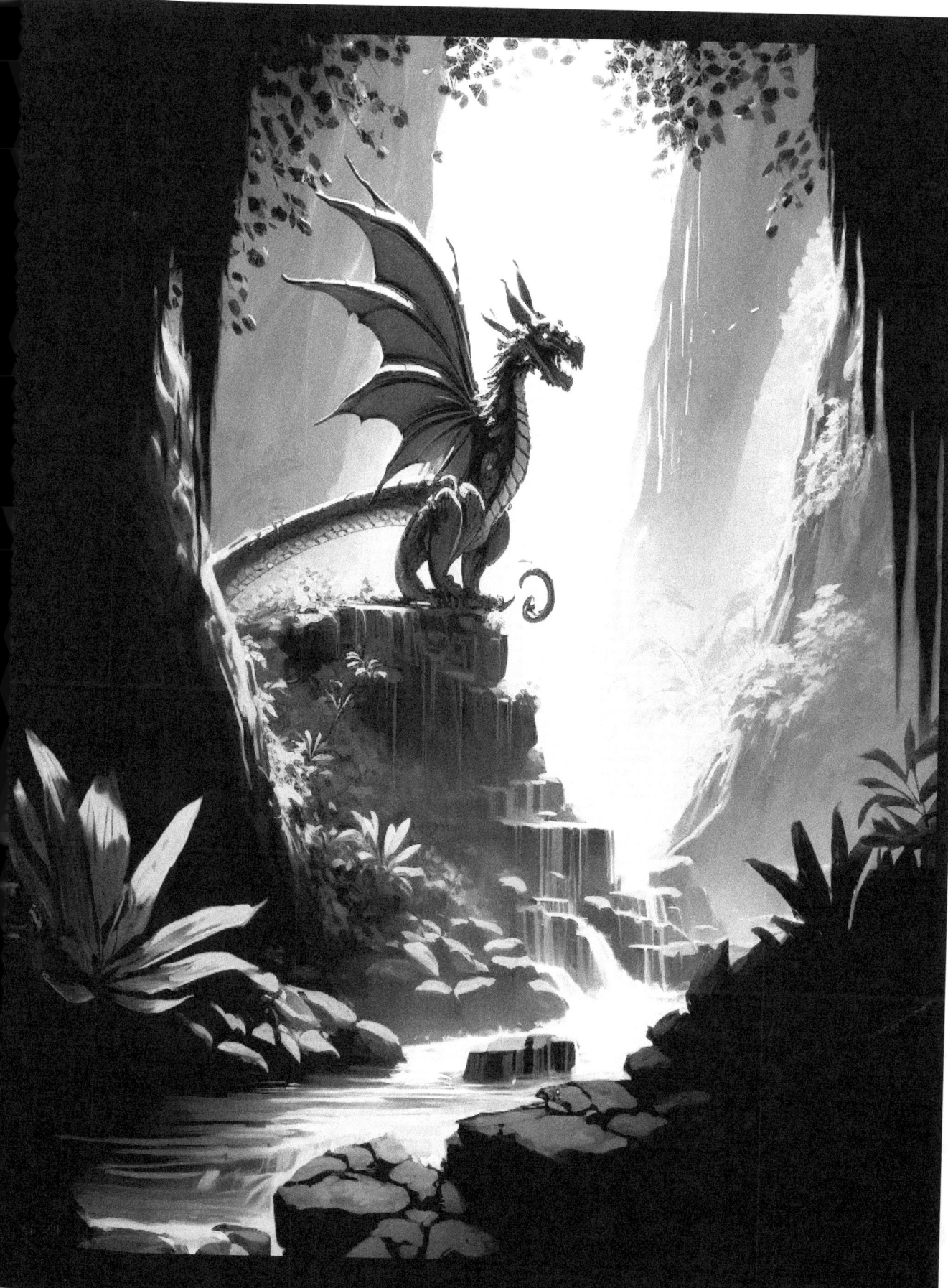

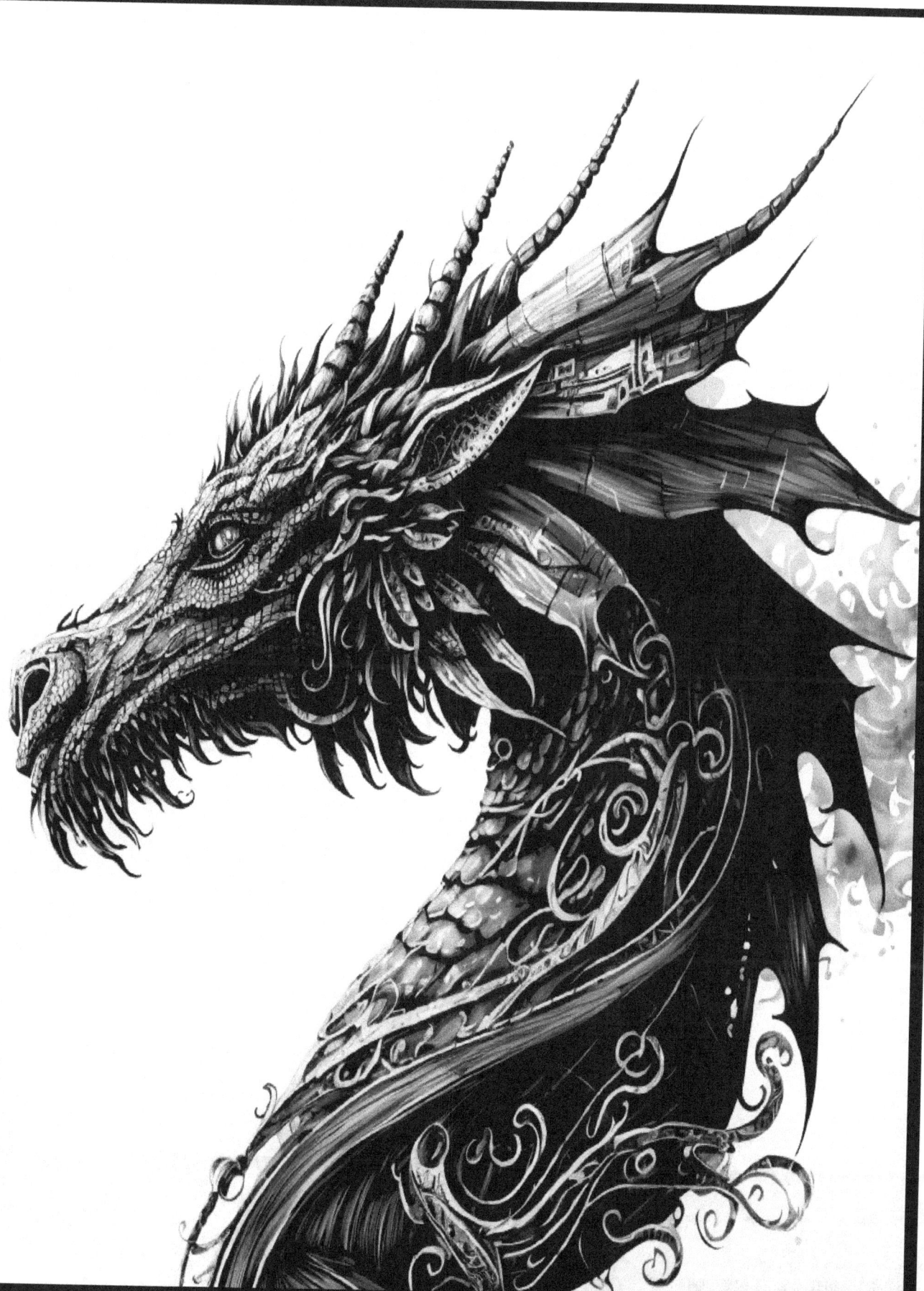

www.ingramcontent.com/pod-product-compliance
Lightning Source LLC
Chambersburg PA
CBHW080442220526
45465CB00007B/2735